GOD'S
Little Rule Book™

*Simple Rules to Bring Joy
and Happiness to Your Life*

STARBURST  PUBLISHERS®

www.starburstpublishers.com

STARBURST PUBLISHERS
P.O. Box 4123, Lancaster, Pennsylvania 17604
www.starburstpublishers.com

Cover art by Richmond and Williams.
Design and composition by John Reinhardt Book Design.

First Printing, November 1999
ISBN: 1-892016-16-8
Library of Congress Catalog Number 99-63790

Printed in the United States of America

Introduction

What is God's Little Rule Book? Think of it as a spiritual supplement providing a healthy "dose" of God's Word for any time of day. Whether you are waiting for a train or walking on a treadmill, God's Little Rule Book will boost your walk with God. Just read the rules and apply the useful "tips" to your own life.

Follow the Rule

Keep training wheels
on your tongue.

Set a guard over my mouth, O Lord;
keep watch over the door of my lips.

PSALM 141:3 NIV

Sticks and stones break bones, but words
can break a heart. The next time you feel anger
and feel the need to vent, consider first
the impact your words will have.

Take a Step

Eat at least three servings
of spiritual fruit daily.

But the fruit of the Spirit is love, joy, peace, patience, kindness, goodness, faithfulness, gentleness, and self-control.

GALATIANS 5:22–23A NIV

Pick three spiritual qualities from the fruit bowl and incorporate them into your day. For example, gentleness could be your morning focus; patience your afternoon portion; and joy your evening dessert!

Take a Step

Go to the Throne,
not to the phone.

*Don't worry about anything; instead,
pray about everything. Tell God what you need,
and thank him for all he has done.*

PHILIPPIANS 4:6 NLT

Instead of running to the phone
to call a friend with your problems,
go to the Lord. He's the only One
who can solve them!

Take a Step

To neutralize burns,
apply blessings.

Bless those who curse you,
pray for those who mistreat you.

LUKE 6:28 NIV

Today during your prayer time,
think of someone whose words
or actions have "burned" you,
and ask God to bless that person.

Take a Step

Follow the Rule

When in doubt, wait it out.

But let patience have its perfect work,
that you may be perfect and complete, lacking nothing.

JAMES 1:4 NKJV

Practice patience. Wait. Pray.
Then wait some more.

Take a Step

Follow the Rule

Love is a verb.

*This is how we know what love is: Jesus Christ
laid down His life for us. And we ought to
lay down our lives for our brothers.*

1 JOHN 3:16 NIV

Do something today that puts the needs
and desires of others before your own needs
and desires.

Take a Step

Follow the Rule

Apologies make
great pillows.

*Don't let the sun go down while you are still angry,
for anger gives a mighty foothold to the Devil.*

EPHESIANS 4:26B–27 NLT

Ever wonder what to write in a wedding card?
This verse is a pearl of wisdom
for any married couple!

Take a Step

Don't stay on your knees
so long that you lose
your ability to walk.

Then the Lord said to Moses, Why are you crying out to me? Tell the people to get moving!

EXODUS 14:15 NLT

There's a time to pray and a time for action.
Don't undertake one without the other.

Take a Step

Follow the Rule

When you join in a tug of war,
expect to get blisters.

He heals the brokenhearted and binds up their wounds.

PSALM 147:3 NIV

Know in advance that Satan is pulling
against you and that living according to God's
standards inevitably leads to hurt and pain.
Don't feel wronged or disappointed
when it happens. Claim God's promise
in Psalm 147 and continue the contest.

Take a Step

Casual promises are like beads strung on air.

*It's better not to make a vow
than to make a vow and not fulfill it.*

Ecclesiastes 5:5 NIV

Consider promises, however minor, contracts.
Avoid promising quickly. Ask first: Do I have the
means, the time, the energy, and the *will* to
deliver? A promise is an appendage of who
we are. Break one, and we sever our validity . . .
and compromise another's portfolio of trust.

Take a Step

Praise is a child's
best vitamin.

And he took the children in his arms,
put his hands on them and blessed them.

MARK 10:16 NIV

Never pass up an opportunity
to give a child a hug, a smile,
or a word of encouragement.

Take a Step

Follow the Rule

Don't flirt with temptation.

Can a man scoop fire into his lap
and not be burned?

PROVERBS 6:27 NLT

Occupy your day with worthy pursuits,
and the Tempter will work on someone
who's not quite so busy.

Take a Step

Follow the Rule

Stay out of mud puddles.

Live such good lives . . . that, though they accuse you
of doing wrong, they may see your good deeds . . .

1 PETER 2:12 NIV

When someone lies about you or in some other
way throws mud at you, don't get in the mud
puddle with them. Live above what they're
saying about you, and others will know the truth.
If you play in mud puddles, you just get dirty.

Take a Step

Follow the Rule

Choose your loves with care.

Above all else, guard your heart, for it affects everything you do.

PROVERBS 4:23 NLT

Make a list of who and what you love.
Consider dropping some and adding others
so your love for God and care for others
take priority.

Take a Step

Follow the Rule

Have a plan and pray with it.

Therefore I do not run like a man running aimlessly; I do not fight like a man beating the air.

1 CORINTHIANS 9:26 NIV

Pray when you list your daily plans.
Ask God to help you prioritize.

Take a Step

Be a giver of second chances.

*Then Peter came to Jesus and asked "Lord, how many
times shall I forgive my brother when he sins against me?
Up to seven times?" Jesus answered, "I tell you,
not seven times, but seventy-seven times."*

MATTHEW 18:21–22 NIV

Make a list of the times you've needed
a second chance. Review the list next time
you need to show forgiveness and mercy.

Take a Step

Only one opinion matters.

We are not trying to please men but God,
who tests our hearts.

1 Thessalonians 2:4b NIV

God doesn't care if you have the best
or worst voice in church. Sing out to him
with joy and adoration on Sunday morning.
He will be pleased and hear nothing
but the purest sounds coming from your heart.

Take a Step

Release your fear,
grab your faith.

He will have no fear of bad news;
his heart is steadfast, trusting in the Lord.

PSALM 112:7 NIV

Write a fear you have on a piece of paper,
fold it and put it in a drawer for one week.
Then take it out, read it, and throw it away.

Take a Step

Follow the Rule

Give money, don't love it.

*For the love of money is at the root of all kinds
of evil. And some people, craving money,
have wandered from the faith and pierced
themselves with many sorrows.*

1 TIMOTHY 6:10 NLT

Look for opportunities to give generously
to others instead of wanting what they have.

Take a Step

Follow the Rule

Honor God with your work,
no matter what it may be.

*Whatever you do, work at it with all your heart,
as working for the Lord, not for men, since you know
that you will receive an inheritance from the Lord
as a reward. It is the Lord Christ you are serving.*

COLOSSIANS 3:23–24 NIV

Make a list of ways you can glorify God through your
work. Include things like having a good attitude,
working hard, being punctual, being courteous,
sharing your faith, and guarding your integrity.

Take a Step

Follow the Rule

Try to "get along" with everyone who "comes along."

If it is possible, as far as it depends on you,
live at peace with everyone.

ROMANS 12:18 NIV

Ask God to fill you with love
for the people who try your patience.

Take a Step

Pass the plate with a smile.

*Each man should give what he has decided
in his heart to give, not reluctantly
or under compulsion, for God loves a cheerful giver.*

2 CORINTHIANS 9:7 NIV

When you give, don't count the cost.

Take a Step

Follow the Rule

Read the instruction manual.

*All Scripture is God-breathed and is useful
for teaching, rebuking, correcting,
and training in righteousness.*

2 TIMOTHY 3:16 NIV

Before you begin a project, read the Bible—
God's instruction manual.

Take a Step

There is a reason
for everything.

*And we know that in all things God works
for the good of those who love him,
who have been called according to his purpose.*

ROMANS 8:28 NIV

Think about where you are in life and how
you got there. Remember experiences
in your past that helped you grow, even though
some may have seemed meaningless at the time.

Take a Step

Be careful with whom you pal around.

The righteous should choose his friends carefully.
For the way of the wicked leads them astray.

PROVERBS 12:26 NKJV

Take a "friend" inventory.
Are your friends drawing you closer to God
or pushing you away from him?

Take a Step

Humility will
get you promoted.

Humble yourselves, therefore, under God's
mighty hand, that he may lift you up in due time.
1 PETER 5:6 NIV

Detecting God's hand
in seeming adversity gives assurance
he will use it for our good.

Take a Step

Follow the Rule

Dumping is allowed.

Cast all your anxiety on him,
because he cares for you.
1 PETER 5:7 NIV

Tell God about the thing that is
weighing heavily on your heart. Inhale deeply,
then exhale your prayer. Ask Him for wisdom,
understanding, and courage.

Take a Step

Follow the Rule

Plan ahead. It wasn't raining
when Noah built the ark.

But the plans of the Lord stand firm forever,
the purposes of his heart through all generations.

PSALM 33:11 NIV

Plan a special occasion and write those plans
on a memo pad. Post it on your computer.

Take a Step

One birthday isn't enough.

You must be born again.
JOHN 3:7B NIV

It makes no difference what church you belong to
or what good things you have done. If you don't
have a spiritual birthday, you don't have a place
in heaven. Stop now and ask Jesus to come
and live in your heart and forgive your sin.

Take a Step

Don't let your words spoil your image.

*Do not let any unwholesome talk come out of
your mouths, but only what is helpful
for building others up according to their needs.*

EPHESIANS 4:29 NIV

Consciously offer each word you speak
as a gift: swathed in kindness,
wrapped in encouragement,
beribboned with appreciation.

Take a Step

Follow the Rule

Don't clutter your life
with old sins.

He who conceals his sins does not prosper,
but whoever confesses and renounces them finds mercy.

PROVERBS 28:13 NIV

Write down your sins daily on the computer.
Confess them to the Lord.
Now hit the delete button. They're gone!

Take a Step

Follow the Rule

Ignorance is always
a voluntary condition.

Study to show thyself approved unto God,
a workman that needeth not to be ashamed,
rightly dividing the word of truth.

2 TIMOTHY 2:15 KJV

Keep a book of short devotionals or a copy of
Scripture verses to learn by your telephone.
While you are waiting "on hold"
spend the minutes replacing one bit
of ignorance with knowledge.

Take a Step

God would rather be our
Guide than hand us a map.

*By day the Lord went ahead of them
in a pillar of cloud to guide them on their way
and by night in a pillar of fire to give them light,
so that they could travel by day or night.*

EXODUS 13:21 NIV

Write down a memory of a time
you've been especially aware of God's presence
as you followed His leading.

Take a Step

Follow the Rule

Be a buddy-builder.

*Therefore encourage one another
and build each other up, just as in fact you are doing.*

1 THESSALONIANS 5:11 NIV

When you discover a loved one's weakness,
instead of criticizing, find a way to build
the person up in that area. Catch a lazy person
working, a messy person cleaning up, or a tardy
person arriving on time and compliment them on
the positive behavior.

Take a Step

Return honey for vinegar.

Do not be overcome by evil,
but overcome evil with good.

ROMANS 12:21 NIV

Determine your freedom to choose—
not who dislikes you, but how you respond
to that dislike. Put those who have wronged you
on your prayer list. Observe how hatred
shrivels in the light of kindness.

Take a Step

If it's worth fighting for,
try diplomacy first.

Don't get into needless fights.
PROVERBS 3:30 TLB

Before engaging in battle,
always consider the goal, the cost,
the necessity, and the alternatives.

Take a Step

Follow the Rule

Share your blessings.

Selling their possessions and goods,
they gave to anyone as he had need.

ACTS 2:45 NIV

Go through a closet or drawer
and choose something to give away.

Take a Step

Follow the Rule

Keep your friends;
keep a silent tongue.

A troublemaker plants seeds of strife;
gossip separates the best of friends.

PROVERBS 16:28 NLT

Make it a habit to forget words of gossip
as soon as they enter your ear.

Take a Step

Follow the Rule

Make a daily deposit in your
heavenly bank account.

*Do not store up for yourselves treasures on earth,
where moth and rust destroy, and where thieves break in
and steal. But store up for yourselves treasures in heaven,
where moth and rust do not destroy, and where thieves
do not break in and steal.*

MATTHEW 6:19 NIV

Write an encouraging letter
to a struggling person.
God can give your words eternal value.

Take a Step

God, your Provider,
will never declare bankruptcy.

And this same God who takes care of me
will supply all your needs from his glorious riches,
which have been given to us in Christ Jesus.

PHILIPPIANS 4:19 NLT

Learn to trust God for small needs
as well as the large.

Take a Step

Follow the Rule

Don't overstate your point.

*The more the words, the less the meaning,
and how does that profit anyone?*

ECCLESIASTES 6:11 NIV

Be honest, and you won't have to
make your point over and over again.
Truth will speak for itself.

Take a Step

Choose your battles wisely.

Don't have anything to do with foolish and stupid arguments, because you know they produce quarrels.

2 TIMOTHY 2:23 NIV

Recite this rhyme and put it into practice:
Learn to stop and count to ten, then,
stop and count to ten, again.

Take a Step

See every day
as a handmade gift.

This is the day the Lord has made;
let us rejoice and be glad in it.

PSALM 118:24 NIV

Giggle with a child. Drink in the rainbow
of God's creation. Smell the peonies.
Sit for fifteen minutes with your feet propped up.
The earth was given for us to enjoy.
So enjoy it! Your soul will be refreshed.

Take a Step

Follow the Rule

Fall asleep talking to God.

On my bed I remember you;
I think of you through the watches of the night.

PSALM 63:6 NIV

When you put your head on the pillow,
review the day with God.

Take a Step

Follow the Rule

Know the Bible.

Do your best to present yourself to God as one approved,
a workman who does not need to be ashamed
and who correctly handles the word of truth.

2 TIMOTHY 2:15 NIV

Don't confuse human literature, superstitions
and folk sayings with the eternal,
inspired word of God.

Take a Step

Know where you're headed.

Where there is no vision, the people perish.
PROVERBS 29:18 KJV

Take the time to get a clear view of where
you are headed. Learning the patience
of waiting may save you
from costly mistakes and dead ends.

Take a Step

Follow the Rule

You can't find buried treasure
without getting your
hands dirty.

. . . and if you call out for insight and cry aloud for understanding, and if you look for it as for silver and search for it as for hidden treasure, then you will understand the fear of the Lord and find the knowledge of God.

PROVERBS 2:3–5 NIV

A good place to start looking for hidden treasure
is directly under your worst circumstances.

When things take a turn for the worst
and you just don't understand . . . start digging.

Take a Step

Follow the Rule

Successful living
requires team players.

Two are better than one, because they have a good return for their work: if one falls down, his friend can help him up, but pity the man who falls and has no one to help him up!

ECCLESIASTES 4:9–10 NIV

Our culture teaches us independence
and individualism, but in God's kingdom
interdependence and community are emphasized.
Think about how you can be a team player today.
Help somebody, but also let him help you.

Take a Step

Follow the Rule

Measure your strength
by your weakness.

Since I know it is all for Christ's good, I am quite content with my weaknesses and with insults, hardships, persecutions, and calamities. For when I am weak, then I am strong.

2 Corinthians 12:10 NLT

The Bible is better than Bally's Health Club
when it comes to building
strength and confidence.
A verse a day keeps the doctor away!

Take a Step

Follow the Rule

Live in the present.

*Forget the former things; do not dwell on the past.
See, I am doing a new thing! Now it springs up;
do you not perceive it? I am making a way in the desert
and streams in the wasteland.*

ISAIAH 43:18–19 NIV

Trust God with your past as well as your future,
and open your eyes to present-day changes
he wants to create for you.

Take a Step

We are called to be a light
to the world—
not a lightning bolt.

Always be prepared to give an answer to everyone who asks you to give the reason for the hope that you have. But do this with gentleness and respect. . . .

1 PETER 3:15B NIV

Let the light of Christ in your life be like a sunrise which draws people by it's warmth, then gently covers them in illumination. People tend to run from lightning bolts.

Take a Step

Love God
with everything you've got.

Love the Lord your God will all your heart
and with all your soul and with all your mind
and with all your strength.

MARK 12:30 NIV

Think about the kind of passion this verse
is talking about. Ask God to fill you
with overwhelming love for him.

Take a Step

Build your house
with the right materials.

By wisdom a house is built, and through understanding it is established; through knowledge its rooms are filled with rare and beautiful treasures.

PROVERBS 24:3–4 NIV

Wisdom, understanding, and knowledge are found in God's Word; read your Bible every day. Then your house will be filled with rare and beautiful treasures.

Take a Step

Follow the Rule

Expect imperfection
in yourself and others.

Be humble and gentle. Be patient with each other,
making allowance for each other's faults
because of your love.

EPHESIANS 4:2 NLT

Be patient with a wrongdoer.
Speak softly to an angry person.
Admit your faults.

Take a Step

Follow the Rule

Make it a practice
to give things away secretly.

But when you give to the needy, do not let your left hand know what your right hand is doing, so that your giving may be in secret.

MATTHEW 6:3–4 NIV

Secretly leave money in someone's Bible, pocketbook, or under their door. Don't run home and tell your family or anyone else what you've done. Let it be between you and God.

Take a Step

Follow the Rule

You are what you think.

Finally, brothers, whatever is true, whatever is noble,
whatever is right, whatever is pure, whatever is lovely,
whatever is admirable—if anything is excellent
or praiseworthy—think about such things.

PHILIPPIANS 4:8 NIV

Concentrate on the positive:
it's a healthy habit.

Take a Step

Angels are seldom seen
wearing halos
and sporting wings.

Do not forget to entertain strangers,
for by so doing some people have entertained angels
without knowing it.

HEBREWS 13:2 NIV

Be generous with food for the heart and soul.

Take a Step

Follow the Rule

Love the unlovable.

You have heard that the law of Moses says,
'Love your neighbor' and hate your enemy.
But I say, love your enemies!
Pray for those who persecute you!

MATTHEW 5:43 NLT

Every day someone benefits from your
compassionate attempt to show God's love.

Take a Step

Follow the Rule

Don't be afraid
to jump ship.

"Lord, if it's you," Peter replied, *"tell me to come to you on the water." "Come,"* he said. *Then Peter got down out of the boat, walked on the water and came toward Jesus.*

MATTHEW 14:28–29 NIV

Dare to ask God where he wants you to follow him today.

Take a Step

Follow the Rule

Look at interruptions
as opportunities from God.

But Jesus called the children to him and said, "Let the little children come to me, and do not hinder them, . . ."

LUKE 18:16A NIV

Interruptions present some of the best opportunities to comfort others and show them grace and compassion. Take those times to be like Jesus and "do not hinder them."

Take a Step

God can use anybody.

*When they saw the courage of Peter and John
and realized that they were unschooled, ordinary men,
they were astonished and they took note
that these men had been with Jesus.*

ACTS 4:13 NIV

Take a walk with Jesus in the Bible every day,
and people will see a change in you.

Take a Step

Follow the Rule

Always tell the truth,
but be diplomatic about it.

*Let love and faithfulness never leave you; bind them
around your neck, write them on the tablet of your heart.*

PROVERBS 3:3 NIV

You have no control over what the truth is,
but you can control how you relay it. Use gentle
words, and if the truth hurts, offer support
and encouragement. Never forget that "truthful"
and "kind" are meant to go hand-in-hand.

Take a Step

Don't get caught up
in a love triangle
with God and money.

No one can serve two masters. Either he will hate the one and love the other, or he will be devoted to the one and despise the other. You cannot serve both God and money.

MATTHEW 6:24 NIV

Take an inventory of your time.
How many hours a week do you spend thinking about your finances? How does that amount compare to the time you spend with God?

Take a Step

Choose an attitude
of gratitude.

No matter what happens, always be thankful, for this is God's will for you who belong to Christ Jesus.

1 THESSALONIANS 5:18 NLT

Whisper one grateful thought once when you rise, and once when you retire. Slowly begin to fill in the rest of the day until your natural attitude is gratitude.

Take a Step

Never underestimate
the power of gentle words.

Through patience a ruler can be persuaded,
and a gentle tongue can break a bone.

PROVERBS 25:15 NIV

Recheck yourself throughout each day
to see if your words have been gentle.
Always be mindful of the power they hold.

Take a Step

Follow the Rule

Always remember whose—
not who—you are.

For in him we live and move and have our being. . . .
ACTS 17:28 NIV

Listen for the voices that define your identity.
Then choose to believe what God says
about you—not what others say.

Take a Step

Follow the Rule

Get your priorities
in proper order.

*But seek first his kingdom and his righteousness,
and all these things will be given to you as well.*

MATTHEW 6:33 NIV

When looking for a job, it is more important
to ask how it will fit into God's plan for your
inner life than to ask how much money it pays.

Take a Step

Treat your mind as if it were a country club with an exclusive membership.

Therefore, holy brothers, who share in the heavenly calling, fix your thoughts on Jesus, the apostle and high priest whom we confess.

HEBREWS 3:1 NIV

Imagine that your thoughts
are things you are saying to Jesus.
How often would your words hurt him?

Take a Step

Starve a grudge;
feed an enemy.

If your enemy is hungry, feed him; if he is thirsty, give him something to drink. . . .

ROMANS 12:20 NIV

Ask the person who has offended you, "What is your favorite food?" Then bring it to him with a smile and a "God bless you." Repeat as necessary. Soon resentment will melt away.

Take a Step

Follow the Rule

Listen twice as much
as you speak.

He who answers before listening—
that is his folly and his shame.

Proverbs 18:13 NIV

Concentrate on your listening skills
by giving someone your full attention with good
eye contact. Ask thoughtful questions
to make sure you understand the meaning
of what is being said.

Take a Step

Follow the Rule

Three components of
spiritual growth are: prayer,
scripture, and reflection.

Like newborn babies, crave pure spiritual milk,
so that by it you may grow up in your salvation.

1 PETER 2:2 NIV

Deepen your faith by talking to God every day.
Study a biblical character. Pray that God will
show you how that person's story
is relevant today.

Take a Step

Follow the Rule

Clear your plans
with the Boss first.

Commit to the Lord whatever you do,
and your plans will succeed.

PROVERBS 16:3 NIV

Don't waste your time making plans
that will have to be changed later.
Commit it to the Lord
and let him clear a path for you.

Take a Step

It's not your place
to put others in their place.

*When they hurled their insults at him [Jesus], he did not
retaliate; when he suffered, he made no threats.
Instead, he entrusted himself to him who judges justly.*

1 PETER 2:23 NIV

We like to make sure that people who mistreat us
don't get away with it. Resist an overly strong
desire to make them pay, and remember that our
righteous judge sees everything.

Take a Step

Follow the Rule

If you want to get somewhere,
stay close to God.

For the Lord watches over the path of the godly,
but the path of the wicked leads to destruction.

PSALMS 1:6 NLT

Begin with prayer, commit new endeavors
to the Lord, take the steps that seem right
and good, and keep the long view—it's not
this earth that's the goal, but eternity.

Take a Step

Don't hook your caboose
to just any engine.

My child, if sinners entice you, turn your back on them!
PROVERBS 1:10 NLT

The world is full of many who would pull you off track. Before you embark, find out where the train is headed.

Take a Step

Contributors

Arthurs, L. Elizabeth, 668 N. Bullmoose Dr., Chandler, AZ 85224.
    Kc7sko@aol.com. [36]
Bandy, Esther, 51 E. Tregaron Ct., Shelton, WA 98584. ebandy@juno.com. [38]
Bell, Kelly, 41789 Asteroid Way, Temecula, CA 92592.
    kbell@ccmurrieta.com. [42, 48, 50]
Benfield, LeAnne E., 1007 Lansfaire Crossing, Suwanee, GA 30024.
    lbenfield@mindspring.com. [40]
Bergh, Ellen, 3600 Brabham Ave., Rosamond CA 93560-6891.
    mastermedia@hughes.net. [2]
Blanchard, Brenda, 7511 Sutters Mine, Converse, TX 78109.
    ZBGP1@aol.com. [32]
Boyll, Cindy Schaible, 10080 Morgan's Trace Dr., Loveland, OH 45140.
    aerywing@xu.campuscwix.net. [4, 96, 100, 130, 140]
Capen, Rosemary Lemcool, 560 SE 27 Lane, Homestead, FL 33033-5214.
    RLCapen@aol.com. [28, 108]
Creasman, Elaine, 13014-106th. Ave. N, Largo, FL 33774-5602.
    emcreasman@aol.com. [68, 110, 138]
Cunningham, Elaine, 1008 Wedgewood Ave., Wenatchee, WA 98801.
    elainecunn@aol.com. [46]

Duncan, Sylvia, 6216 Potomac St., St. Louis, MO 63139. [30]

Engles, Doris D., 235 Allenberry Circle, Pittsburgh, PA 15234. howard@nb.net. [116]

Fugman, Jan, 2416 SW 23rd Circle, Troutdale, OR 97060. [44, 114]

Gilden, Linda J., 105 Pheasant Dr., Spartanburg, SC 29302. Rosewriter@aol.com. [22]

Gonzales, Judith M., 1108 W. Rose Ave., Moses Lake, WA 98837-2062. jmg.sp.ink@juno.com. [104, 134]

Hampton, Judy, 670 Oakhaven Ave., Brea, CA 92823. judyjudyjudy9@Juno.com. [6, 120]

Healton, Sarah, 6669 Belinda Dr., Riverside, CA 92504. [56]

Hopler, Whitney Von Lake, 3 Asbury Way, Sterling, VA 20165. WhitneyVLH@aol.com. [66, 126]

Hudson, Lois, 17921 Romelle Ave., Santa Ana, CA 92705. James.Hudson3@gte.net. [60]

Humber, Armené, 11166 McGee River Circle, Fountain Valley, CA 92708. armhumber@aol.com. [8, 128, 132]

Irby, Elizabeth, 6199 SE Heike St., Hillsboro, OR 97123. elizabeth.irby@hevanet.com. [142]

Jadlow, Sally, 10802 W. 102 St., Overland Park, KS 66214. Sjadlow@aol.com. [58]

Kesinger, Helen E., 221 Brookside Dr., Paola, KS 66071. kesinger@micoks.net. [62, 122, 144]

Kuoni, Helene C., 10 North Brook Ave., Basking Ridge, NJ 07920. jkuoni@erols.com. [16, 24, 72, 124, 148, 150]

Malroy, Rosemarie D., 10413 N. Demaret Dr., Fountain Hills, AZ 85268. RMalroy@aol.com. [34]

Marbaugh, Ruth A., 205 London Rd., Hendersonville, NC 28739. [18, 64]

Miholer, Sue, 1075 Willow Lake Road N., Salem, OR 97303. miholer@viser.net. [26]

Minshull, Evelyn, 724 Airport Rd., Mercer, PA 16137. eminshull@juno.com. [20, 70]

Moore, Phylis, 2457 Mattison Lane, Santa Cruz, CA 95062. pjmoore@cruzers.net. [74]

Phelps, Vickie, P.O. Box 5907, Longview, Texas 75608. V1950phel@aol.com. [80]

Plaep, David R., 8001 Jefferson St., Spring Lake Park, MN 55432. daveplaep@timberbay.org. [54, 118, 136, 146]

Potter, Betty, 39600 Crawfordsville Dr., Sweet Home, OR 97386. [76]

Robertson, Robbie, 4546 East Maya Way, Cave Creek, AZ 85331-6684. [82]

Rollings, Lucinda J., 3867 West Fairview Rd., Greenwood, IN 46142. awana.ec.ind@juno.com. [86]

Rose, Penny Pierce, 6529 Esther NE, Albuquerque, NM 87109.
  Prose4H@aol.com. [10]
Schmidt, Doug, Senior Editor, David C. Cook Publishing Co.
  www.dougschmidt.com. [88]
Standerfer, Carolyn, 4847 W. Ave. N, Quartz Hill, CA 93536-2465.
  carolyns@hughes.net. [94, 102]
Thompson, Gail Woods, 4069 Salem Farm Road, Oxford, North Carolina
  27565. Gailsong@aol.com, UglyOleDog@aol.com. [84, 112]
Thompson, Jane Foard, 3206 Teal Ave., Sarasota, FL 34232.
  janesara@home.com. [92]
Velia, Ann M., 4248 Mission Bell Ave., Las Cruces, NM 88011-9610,
  jvelia@zianet.com. [90]
Waldon, Marja, 2821 E. 36th Ct., Des Moines, IA 50317, parj@juno.com.
  [12, 106]
Walton, Elizabeth C., Rose Villa Retirement Community, 13505 SE River
  Road, Portland, OR 97222. ecwalt@teleport.com. [52]
Wilt, Elizabeth Marie, 16708 George Franklyn Dr., Independence, MO
  64055. elizabethmwilt@dupontpharma.com.[14, 78, 98]

Other Books by Starburst Publishers

**God's Little Rule Book: Simple Rules to Bring Joy
and Happiness to Your Life**
Starburst Publishers

Let this little book of God's rules be your personal guide to a more joyful life.
Brimming with easily applicable rules, this book is sure to inspire and motivate
you! Each rule includes corresponding scripture and a practical tip that will
help to incorporate God's rules into everyday life. Simple enough to fit into a
busy schedule, yet powerful enough to be life changing!
(trade paper) ISBN 1892016168 **$6.95**

**Life's Little Rule Book: Simple Rules to Bring Joy
and Happiness to Your Life**
Starburst Publishers

Let this little book inspire you to live a happier life! The pages are filled with
timeless rules such as, "Learn to cook, you'll always be in demand!" and "Help
something grow." Each rule is combined with a reflective quote and a simple
suggestion to help the reader incorporate the rule into everyday life.
(trade paper) ISBN 1892016176 **$6.95**